LAW CARTOONS

AUSTRALIA
The Law Book Company
Brisbane • Sydney • Melbourne • Perth

CANADA
Carswell
Ottawa • Toronto • Calgary • Montreal • Vancouver

AGENTS
Steimatzky's Agency Ltd., Tel Aviv;
N.M. Tripathi (Private) Ltd., Bombay;
Eastern Law House (Private) Ltd., Calcutta;
M.P.P. House, Bangalore;
Universal Book Traders, Delhi;
Aditya Books, Delhi;
MacMillan Shuppan KK, Tokyo;
Pakistan Law House, Karachi, Lahore

LAW CARTOONS

by

Susan Tayfoor, LL.B.

Lecturer, Birkbeck College

First Edition

London
Sweet & Maxwell
1995

Published in 1995 by
Sweet & Maxwell Limited
of South Quay Plaza,
183 Marsh Wall, London E14 9FT

Printed in Great Britain by The Headway Press Ltd.

A CIP catalogue record for this book
is available from the British Library

ISBN 0421 544 708

A Foreword...

The Characters in Criminal Law:

The Accused
(or defendant) is the
person charged with
an offence

The Prosecutor
is the person taking
proceedings in the name
of the Crown

The Judge
(or magistrate)
has the power to
sentence the accused

Warning!

This book is not intended as a legal
bible. If you are thinking of conducting
your own court case, you would be
advised to supplement your reading
with a sturdy textbook.

CONTENTS

GLOSSARY OF SOME LEGAL TERMS

ACCUSED — The accused (or the defendant) is the person who is charged with the offence.

ACTUS REUS — The actus reus is the physical element of the crime, the act which constitutes the crime - e.g. holding up a gun and shooting someone.

ACQUITTAL — This is when the defendant is found not guilty

AUTOMATISM — This is a defence where the defendant must prove they had no voluntary control over their muscles.

CONSPIRACY — With the exception of conspiracy to defraud and conspiracy to corrupt public morals, this is a statutory offence, existing when two or more persons agree on a course of action which will result in a crime.

DIMINISHED RESPONSIBILITY — This is a defence specifically for a charge of murder, where the accused must show they were suffering from an abnormality of mind which made them not fully responsible for their actions.

DOLI INCAPAX — "Incapable of crime" - a child under ten is presumed to be incapable of committing a crime.

DURESS	This is a defence where the accused must show they were forced to commit the crime as a result of illegal threats
INTENTION	The accused can be said to have intended the consequences if he foresaw them as a virtual certainty .
MENS REA	This is the mental element of the crime - e.g. having the intention to kill someone (murder) or being reckless as to whether they die (manslaughter)
M'NAGHTEN RULES	The M'Naghten rules were formulated in the case R.v M'Naghten 1843, to decide whether a person was not guilty by reason of insanity
NOVUS ACTUS INTERVENIENS	This means that a new, intervening act breaks the chain of causation between the defendant's act and its consequences
PROOF	The burden of proof is on the prosecution to prove beyond reasonable doubt the guilt of the accused .
RECKLESSNESS	Recklessness can be of a 'Cunningham' type, where the defendant deliberately takes a risk, or of the 'Caldwell' type where the defendant may not be aware of the risk involved, but a reasonable man would .

X

Special Types of Offences

Strict Liability Offences

These are offences where it is no defence for the defendant to show he didn't realise certain facts which made his act illegal. He may be convicted even if he didn't intend to commit a crime, or wasn't reckless or negligent in any way.

eg. some road traffic offences   crimes of polluting the environment

Crimes of Specific Intent

A crime of specific intent is one where the prosecution must show an intention to commit the crime. This type of crime can't be committed carelessly, or accidentally.

eg.   murder   Wounding with intent (section 18)   Robbery   Burglary

Intoxication may be a defence to these crimes.

Crimes of Basic Intent

A crime of basic intent may be committed recklessly,

eg.   manslaughter   Wounding under section 20   assault

Intoxication will not be a defence to these crimes.

CHAPTER ONE - THE NATURE OF A CRIME

What is a crime?

> A crime is an unlawful act or default which is an offence against the public and renders the person guilty of the act liable to legal punishment.
>
> Halsbury's Laws of England

Is every 'wrong' a crime?

Not necessarily...

> The great leading rule of criminal law is that nothing is a crime unless it is plainly forbidden by law.

This principle is called "Nullem crimen sine lege"

Who creates new crimes?

This question was debated in the case <u>Shaw v. DPP 1961</u>

One side said only Parliament could make new laws...

> Where Parliament fears to tread, it is not for the courts to rush in

The other side said the courts could create new crimes, when it was necessary to protect the moral welfare of the state.

 How are criminal offences classified?

The Criminal Law Act 1967, s. 1 divides offences into
— INDICTABLE offences
— SUMMARY offences

Indictable offences are more serious crimes tried in the Crown Court

Certain crimes are triable only on indictment, e.g.
— murder
— rape
— blackmail
— robbery

Summary offences are less serious crimes, tried in the Magistrates Court.

 I have no right to a jury.

These include petty driving offences or drunkenness.

Offences triable-either-way

Some offences can be serious, or not-so-serious.
For example, theft...

baked beans — I would be tried in the magistrates court.

Swag — I would be tried in the crown court.

The Police and Criminal Evidence Act 1984

This act divides offences into...

Non-Arrestable Offences

eg. petty driving offences

If I want to arrest someone for these offences, I need a warrant to do so.

Arrestable Offences

e.g. Treason
        murder
     Piracy

(Crimes with at least a 5 year sentence for a first offender over 21 years.)

For these offences, I can arrest someone without a warrant.

Serious Arrestable Offences

eg. carrying firearms with criminal intent
        murder
     serious harm to state security

If a serious arrestable offence is committed, special police powers can be used.

These include road checks, or delaying access to a lawyer.

To convict someone of a crime, I must prove beyond reasonable doubt that the defendant committed that crime, and that they have no valid defence.

'Beyond reasonable doubt' is the standard of proof in criminal cases, for the prosecution.

When I want to prove something, for example that I killed someone in self defence, I must show it is more likely than not that what I say is true.

The standard of proof is lower than that for the prosecution.

If their defence is more likely than not to be true, the prosecution has not proved their case beyond reasonable doubt, and cannot convict them.

The punishment for a crime may be . . .

 Imprisonment

> I've been sentenced to ten years, but I may be released on parole after serving half my sentence.

A suspended sentence

> If I commit a further offence during this time, my prison sentence comes into action.

or Community sentences

Such as a probation order

or community service
(e.g. doing gardening for the elderly)

The defendant may be ordered to pay a fine, or compensation to the victim

> If I'm lucky, I may get an absolute discharge, which means I'm convicted of the offence, but I receive no punishment.

Elements of a crime

"But it was an accident!"

If you commit a criminal act unintentionally, the general rule is that you cannot be guilty of a crime.

Actus non facit reum nisi mens sit rea

This means that the act itself does not make a man guilty, unless his mind is also guilty

There are two parts, then, to a crime :

The physical element — e.g. the act of killing someone
The mental element — e.g. intending to kill them.

The physical element is called the ACTUS REUS
The mental element is referred to as the MENS REA

Usually, both must be present, and must coincide.

So if I decide to kill someone, and accidentally run them over while I'm driving to their house, will I have committed murder?

No, there was no mens rea, at the time the accident happened.

QUIZ - THE NATURE OF A CRIME

① Offences which are triable-either-way depend on the severity of the crime, as to which court they're heard in.

True / False ?

② A police officer can never arrest someone for a non-arrestable offence

True / False ?

③ Taking something which belongs to another is the actus reus (physical element) of theft.

True / False ?

④ If a man dishonestly takes money which he thinks belongs to someone else, he has committed no crime if he finds he was entitled to it anyway, since there is the mens rea, but no actus reus of a crime.

True / False ?

⑤ If someone commits both the actus reus and the mens rea of an offence, they will be guilty of the crime.

True / False ?

CHAPTER TWO - ACTUS REUS

The actus reus is the physical element of the crime

> eg. The actus reus of <u>murder</u> is the unlawful killing of a person, who must die within a year and a day.

The act must be shown to have caused the result, and any intervening event may break this chain of events...

Intending to murder his mother, the defendant prepared her a drink made with cyanide

Come drink your 'nectar', mother

Thank you, dear.

Before she touched the drink, she died - from heart failure

The defendant cannot be convicted of murder, since the victim's death was not due to the poison he gave her.

R.v. White 1910

In <u>R.v. Blaue 1975</u>, the defendant stabbed a Jehovah's Witness, who, because of her religious beliefs, refused a blood transfusion and died.

Did my act cause her death, if she could have been saved otherwise?

Yes. You must take the victim as you find them. She died as a result of the stab wounds

Can you ever commit a crime by failing to act?

Usually, no. You will have committed no crime by simply watching someone drown.

However, certain people may be criminally liable for failing to act ...

Parent →

I was looking after him.

and I pushed him in, in the first place

If you bring about a certain situation, you may be liable for failing to avert the consequences of that act

A squatter fell asleep with a lit cigarette, which set fire to the mattress.
When he woke up, instead of putting the fire out, he simply moved to another room.

Had he committed a crime by not putting the fire out?

Yes, because he had begun the chain of events which resulted in the fire.

R. v. Miller 1983

Sometimes, the actus reus alone can constitute a crime, even though the defendant had no criminal intention

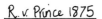
R. v. Prince 1875

The defendant was charged with taking a girl under 16 out of her parents' possession...

But she told me she was 18!

It made no difference that the defendant had reasonably believed she was 18. Doing the act was enough.

If anyone does this wrong act, he does it at the risk of the girl turning out to be under 16.

These types of offences are called crimes of strict liability

A crime can also be committed without mens rea, when a particular situation arises

Police? Please remove this drunk man from the hospital.

hic

The defendant was removed, and taken to a police car outside, where he was charged with being found drunk on the highway.

The defendant was found guilty, even though he'd been taken there by the police and had acted involuntarily.

Winzar v. Chief Constable of Kent 1983

QUIZ - ACTUS REUS

1. X stabbed Y in a fight, and Y was taken to hospital. A few days before he was due to leave, Y was given some drugs he was allergic to, and died. X was responsible for Y's death, since it was because of X that Y was in hospital.

    True / False ?

2. X accidentally drives his car onto a policeman's foot. When he realises, he decides to leave the car there, and switches off the engine. X can argue that he committed no crime, since at the time of the actus reus (driving onto the foot), he had no mens rea, and both must coincide for a crime.

    True / False ?

3. A gunman, being chased by armed police holds a girl hostage in front of him, as a shield, to prevent being shot. The police shoot at him, and kill the girl. He is not responsible for her death, since their shooting was an intervening act.

    True / False ?

4. A man took in his sister, who was suffering from anorexia. She refused to eat, and became unable to move. The man and his housekeeper left her to die, without calling in a doctor. They weren't guilty, however, for an omission to act.

    True / False ?

CHAPTER THREE - MEN'S REA

To be guilty of a criminal act, you usually need to be blameworthy in some way. This "guilty" state of mind is known as mens rea.

Criminal law is about the right of the state to punish wicked persons for their conduct...

Lord Diplock

Treacy v. D.P.P. 1971

A person's motives may not always be bad, however...

I steal from the rich, to give to the poor

This does not mean you are not guilty of the crime. Motive is irrelevant.

Intending to do the act may be enough to constitute a crime, if that act is forbidden by law

But I didn't realise it was illegal!

Ignorance of the law is no excuse!

R. v. Esop 1836

Mens Rea can consist
of various states of mind

- Intention
- Recklessness
- Negligence
- Blameless inadvertence

The mens rea for one crime may be different to another.
For example, manslaughter can be committed negligently, but not murder.

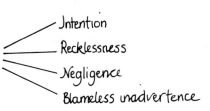

In general, the more serious the crime, the higher degree of mens rea needs to be shown.

Intention

Can X be said to have <u>intended</u> to kill Y if he just wanted to <u>frighten</u> him, or injure him?

The court may infer a result is intended, if the consequences are virtually certain, and the defendant knew this result was virtually certain.

<u>Recklessness</u>.

I fired the gun without checking whether it was loaded or not.

Recklessness is doing an act without paying attention to the obvious risks involved. There are two types of recklessness ...

<u>Cunningham Recklessness</u> : Deliberately taking an unjustified risk, which you are aware of —

When I broke into the gas meter, I pulled a gas pipe off the wall, and didn't care whether the gas escaped.

It did escape, and poisoned the woman next door.

You are guilty of maliciously endangering life, because you deliberately took a risk, and didn't care about the consequences.

<u>R v. Cunningham 1957</u>

<u>Caldwell Recklessness</u> : Creating an obvious risk which you may not be aware of, but which a reasonable man would be.

I set fire to a hotel, but I was so drunk, it never crossed my mind that anyone would be in danger.

Guilty. Recklessness in this type of offence consists of creating an obvious risk, which you either didn't think about, or you went on to do it anyway.

R.v. Caldwell 1982

A person is reckless when they don't give thought to an obvious risk.

What if they consider the risk first?

When I karate-kicked the window, I carefully aimed to miss it by 2 inches.

Unfortunately, he misjudged.

Was he still reckless if he'd considered the risk, and minimised it?

Yes, because he still realised there was some risk involved.

<u>Chief Constable of Avon v. Shimmen 1987</u>

Whether or not the risk is obvious, is measured by the standard of a reasonable man, not whether the risk is obvious to the defendant:

I'm 14, and mentally backward, and I truly didn't realise that lighting a fire to warm myself up would burn the whole shed down.

But a reasonable person would, so you are guilty of arson.

<u>Elliott v. C 1983</u>

Negligence

A person is negligent if he
fails to exercise such care,
skill or foresight as a reasonable
man in his situation would exercise

Law Commission
Report, No. 89

Can you be criminally liable
for negligently causing someone's
death?

Yes, if it amounts to
gross negligence.

Blameless Inadvertence

I gave drugs out on this prescription,
but unknown to me, it was forged.

The pharmacist could not have known the prescription
was forged. He was not blameworthy in any way, and
yet he was convicted of an offence.

This type of crime is a strict liability offence

Pharmaceutical Society of Great Britain v. Storkwain Ltd 1986

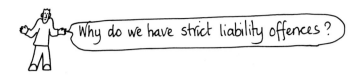 Why do we have strict liability offences?

To protect the public interest. In the words of Lord Diplock...

 The usual justification for creating by statute a criminal offence of strict liability... is the threat that the actus reus of the offence poses to public health, public safety, public morals or public order.

R. v Lemon 1979

Examples of strict liability offences include . . .

- polluting a river

- Selling liquor to a drunken person (Cundy v. Le Cocq 1884)

- selling a tin of peas, with a little caterpillar inside (Smedleys v. Breed 1974)

- Wearing 'foetus earrings' and outraging public decency (R.v. Gibson 1990)

Strict liability offences are sometimes referred to as 'quasi-crimes', meaning they are not morally reprehensible in the same way as crimes such as murder or rape.

QUIZ - MEN'S REA

① The defendant was charged with committing a strict liability offence, made unlawful by a statute passed when he was away at sea. He had no way of knowing about this statute, could be still be guilty of the offence?

Yes / No ?

② A man kills his young son, who is suffering from an incurable illness, and is in great pain. The man will not be guilty of murder, since he doesn't have a criminal intention.

True / False ?

③ 'Intending' to do something is the same as 'wanting' to do it.

True / False ?

④ If the word 'reckless' is used in the definition of one crime, it will have the same meaning as the word 'reckless' used in the definition of any other crime.

True / False ?

⑤ The defendant beats a man until he presumes he is dead, and then throws the victim over a cliff. The victim, who is still alive, dies of exposure. The defendant is not guilty of murder though, since at the time he had the mens rea, this did not occur at the same time as the death of the victim.

True / False ?

CHAPTER FOUR - THE DEFENCES

General Defences may be pleaded for most types of crimes...

eg. "J was forced to kill him!" — Duress

"After a bottle of vodka, J decided to rob a bank." — Intoxication

"J have no recollection of what happened after J hit my head." — Automatism

also... mistake
insanity
self-defence

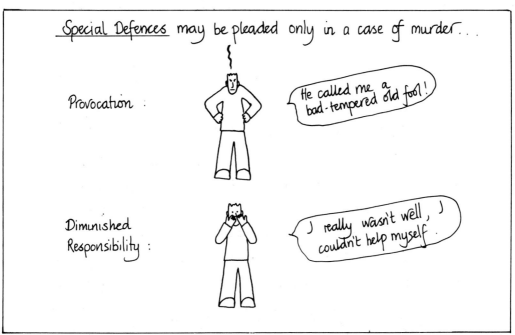

Special Defences may be pleaded only in a case of murder...

Provocation : "He called me a bad-tempered old fool!"

Diminished Responsibility : "J really wasn't well, J couldn't help myself"

Insanity

The definition of insanity is set out in the case R.v. M'Naghten, and known as the M'Naghten Rules:

At the time I committed the act, I was labouring under such a defect of reason, resulting from a disease of the mind, that I didn't know what I was doing, or that it was wrong.

In that case, I find you not guilty, by reason of insanity!

'Disease of the mind' covers illnesses such as

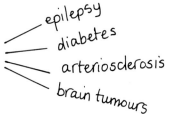

- epilepsy
- diabetes
- arteriosclerosis
- brain tumours

... even sleepwalking has been counted as a disease of the mind

---

Criminal Procedure (Insanity and Unfitness to Plead) Act 1991

Before 1991, when the defence was successful, the judge would order the defendant to be detained indefinitely in a mental hospital.

Now I can give a complete discharge, or an order for treatment or supervision, instead.

Necessity

After a storm at sea, four men were cast adrift in a boat, 1,600 miles from land...

What about the cabin boy down there!

We haven't eaten for days

We'll all die unless we do something!

They killed and ate the cabin boy, and four days later they were rescued, and charged with murder. They pleaded necessity as a defence ...

Circumstances meant we had to kill him. We could all have died otherwise.

The defence was rejected, and they were convicted of murder.

Lord Coleridge CJ.

To preserve one's life is generally speaking a duty, but it may be the plainest and the highest duty to sacrifice it.

R v Dudley and Stephens 1884

Necessity as a defence will not usually excuse the act, but may result in a lower sentence.

Duress

The use of threats and menaces to compel a person, by the fear of death, or grievous bodily harm,... to do some unlawful act or commit a misdemeanour

Blackstone

R v. Hudson and Taylor 1971

We lied in court as witnesses, because we were afraid of a man's threats to us

They had to prove :

1) The threat of violence was real
2) They were so frightened by the threats, that their will was overborne
3) A reasonable person would have reacted this way

They were found not guilty of perjury, since they'd acted under duress

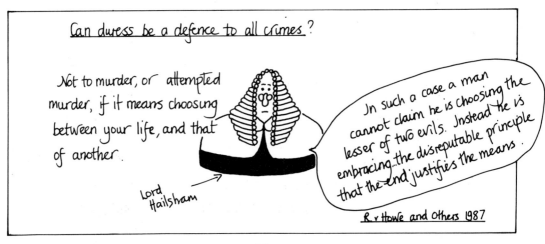

Can duress be a defence to all crimes ?

Not to murder, or attempted murder, if it means choosing between your life, and that of another.

Lord Hailsham

In such a case a man cannot claim he is choosing the lesser of two evils. Instead he is embracing... the disreputable principle that the end justifies the means.

R v Howe and others 1987

22

Automatism

Automatism is when you do an action involuntarily, such as

Lord Denning

> a spasm, a reflex action, or a convulsion, or an act done by a person who is not conscious of what he's doing.

Bratty v. A.G. for Northern Ireland 1963

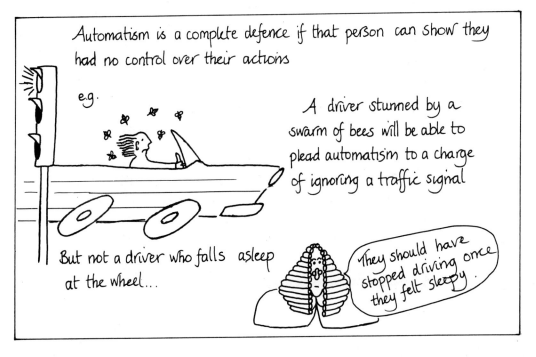

Automatism is a complete defence if that person can show they had no control over their actions

e.g.

A driver stunned by a swarm of bees will be able to plead automatism to a charge of ignoring a traffic signal

But not a driver who falls asleep at the wheel...

> They should have stopped driving once they felt sleepy.

Non-insane automatism is caused by an external event, such as — concussion — a blow on the head

The plea may be insane automatism, if it arises from internal causes such as — epilepsy — diabetes — sleepwalking

23

Self Defence

> I can use self defence to protect myself, provided it's reasonable.

Self defence will be a valid defence, if the act was done to prevent a crime...

or to protect property...

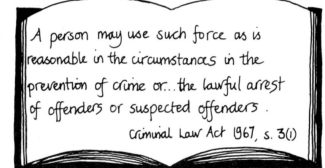

A person may use such force as is reasonable in the circumstances in the prevention of crime or... the lawful arrest of offenders or suspected offenders.

Criminal Law Act 1967, s. 3(1)

The force used must not be excessive, but must be reasonable in the circumstances, as that person perceived them to be:

Mistake

But it's not illegal where I'm from.

A mistake as to law, will be no defence to a crime.

A mistake as to facts may be a defence ...

When it means the defendant didn't have the necessary mens rea for the crime :

I can only rape someone who is not consenting, and I'm aware of this. I mistakenly believed the woman was consenting

D.P.P. v. Morgan 1976

Or in certain cases, if it was a reasonable mistake to make :

My husband was lost at sea for years, so I remarried, and now he's turned up again!

Her mistake of thinking he was dead was a defence to bigamy, since it was a reasonable mistake to make.

R.v. Tolson 1889

Intoxication

You were reckless to get drunk in the first place

Intoxication may be a defence to crimes of specific intent (eg. murder, theft) but is no defence to crimes of basic intent, where it is enough to show recklessness as mens rea (eg manslaughter, assault)

R. v. Lipman 1970

After taking LSD, the defendant hallucinated that his girlfriend had turned into a giant snake, and killed her...

His intoxicated state means he did not have the mens rea for murder. He is, however, guilty of the lesser charge of manslaughter, since he was reckless to take the drugs in the first place.

Intoxication will not always be a defence to murder :

A husband with a grievance resolved to kill his wife, and bought a knife to do so...

I'll have one for dutch courage

He drank the bottle of whisky before killing her. When charged with murder, he pleaded that he was drunk at the time he killed her.

Intoxication is not a defence to murder, since you'd already planned to kill her, before you started drinking.

Attorney-General for Northern Ireland v. Gallagher 1963

QUIZ - THE DEFENCES

① X joined a gang of robbers, who then forced him to commit an offence. Can X plead duress?

Yes / No ?

② If a driver of a car falls asleep at the wheel and causes an accident while he's asleep, will he be able to plead automatism?

Yes / No ?

③ Unknown to X, his friend laces his drink with alcohol. After drinking it, X goes out and assaults a passerby. Can X plead intoxication as a complete defence?

Yes / No ?

④ The defendant drank a bottle of wine which was much stronger than he believed it to be. If he then went on to commit a crime, could he claim intoxication as a defence?

Yes / No ?

⑤ Someone threatens to injure you next month if you don't carry out a robbery with them. Will you be able to plead duress if you do?

Yes / No ?

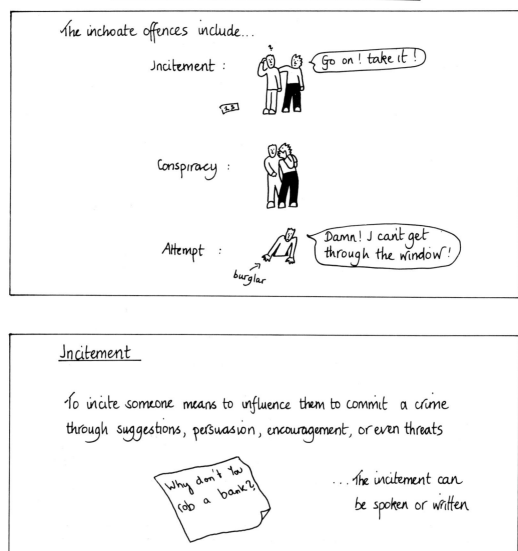

The inchoate offences include...

Incitement :

Conspiracy :

Attempt :

burglar

Incitement

To incite someone means to influence them to commit a crime through suggestions, persuasion, encouragement, or even threats

...The incitement can be spoken or written

It makes no difference if the person being incited carries out the crime or not, the crime of incitement will still be committed

Conspiracy

A conspiracy is an agreement between two or more persons to commit a crime, corrupt public morals, or defraud someone

Conspiracy to Commit a crime

is governed by section 1 of the Criminal Law Act 1977

Conspiracy to corrupt public morals

is a common law offence

I agreed to supply tools for the crime, but I didn't think the plan would work!

You're guilty of conspiracy even if you were sure it wouldn't succeed.

R. v. Anderson 1985

Are there any times I'm not guilty of conspiracy?

Yes, if the only other person you conspire with is ...

... Your spouse

... a child under ten

... or an intended victim

Attempt

> ## The Criminal Attempts Act 1981
>
> If, with intent to commit an offence .. a person does an act which is MORE THAN MERELY PREPARATORY to the commission of the offence, he is guilty of attempting to commit the offence.
>
> s.1.

Attempting an offence can be ...

- lying in wait for the victim

- aiming a gun at someone you intend to shoot

- but not merely buying the gun you intend to shoot someone with.

Can I be convicted of attempting something which turns out to be impossible?

e.g. - trying to steal something which belongs to you

- pickpocketing an empty pocket

Anything to declare?

gulp, no.

D thought he was carrying illegal drugs. They were, in fact, harmless. He was nonetheless convicted of attempting the offence under section 1 (2)

R v. Shivpuri 1987

QUIZ - THE INCHOATE OFFENCES

① A person who incites another to commit an offence, may be punished more severely than the person who actually committed the offence.

True / False ?

② A husband may be guilty of incitement if he encourages his wife to commit a crime.

True / False ?

③ You will have committed no crime if you send a letter, inciting another to commit robbery, if that letter never arrives.

True / False ?

④ The defendant is a company which advertised an instrument for avoiding police speed traps. Could the company be guilty of incitement?

Yes / No ?

⑤ If someone does something which he believes is illegal, but which isn't in fact illegal, will he be guilty of attempt, as he has a criminal intention?

Yes / No ?

CHAPTER SIX · MURDER

Murder is the unlawful killing of a human being, with malice aforethought (the intention to kill or cause really serious injury) and the victim dies within a year and a day.

Intention to kill and the Moloney guidelines

At a wedding anniversary, two men had a race to see who could load a gun first...

On your marks..

Moloney loaded the gun first, pulled the trigger, and shot his stepfather dead.

R.v. Moloney 1985

I didn't have the mens rea for murder. I didn't intend to kill him. It was just a lark.

Lord Bridge set out the guidelines for when intention could be inferred:

Was death a 'natural consequence' of the defendant's act? Did he realise this?

If the answer to both questions is yes, we can assume the defendant intended the consequences of his act.

Later, these guidelines were changed:

We shouldn't ask if the result was a natural consequence of the defendant's act, but rather if it was a virtual certainty

R.v. Nedrick 1986

Provocation

When a defendant is charged with murder, if they can prove they were provoked, they will be convicted, instead, of manslaughter

When can someone plead provocation?

If something the victim did or said, made me lose my self-control and kill them.

The words or acts must be something which would cause a reasonable person to lose their self-control

He whistled at my girlfriend!

The defendant could not claim provocation as a defence.
A reasonable person would not react this way.

There must be no 'cooling-off' period between the words or acts of provocation, and the killing.

I'm fed up with his bullying, now here's my plan.

The killing was premeditated, not done in the heat of the moment.

R. v. Ibrams and Gregory 1981

The defence of provocation is found in the Homicide Act 1957, s. 3

Diminished Responsibility

"I'm on a divine mission from God. I couldn't stop myself."

Diminished responsibility is a defence which can be used only on a charge of murder. If successful, the defendant will be convicted instead of manslaughter.

Where a party kills... another he shall not be convicted of murder if he was suffering from such abnormality of mind... as substantially impaired his mental responsibility for his acts and omissions

Homicide Act 1957, s.2

"abnormality of mind" covers situations such as

- depression
- alcoholism
- "mercy-killings"
- psychopathic disorders
- irresistible impulses

In the case of insanity, the defendant does not realise that what they did was legally wrong. Diminished responsibility is different :

"I knew that what I was doing was wrong, but I just couldn't help myself."

R.v. Byrne 1960

QUIZ - MURDER

① To convict someone of murder, the prosecution needs to show an intention to kill, and nothing less will suffice .

True / false ?

② Provocation will also be a defence to manslaughter.

True / false ?

③ Words can never be enough to count as provocation .

True / false ?

④ X throws a stone, aiming at a person. He misses, however, and breaks a window. He will be guilty of damaging the window, since the mens rea for the offence will be transferred .

True / false ?

⑤ In a fit of anger, a man killed his friend, and pleaded the defence of provocation, saying that he was suffering from depression at the time . However, his depression would not be taken into account when judging whether a reasonable man would react in this way .

True / false ?

CHAPTER SEVEN - MANSLAUGHTER

Manslaughter can be divided into :

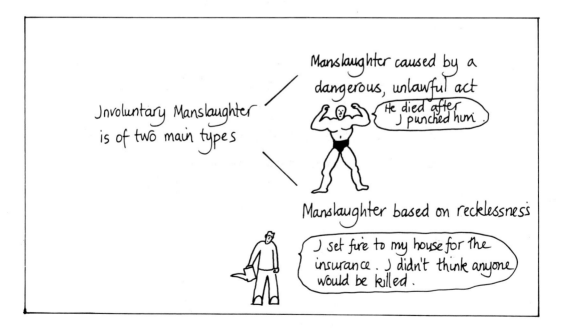

Unlawful Act Manslaughter

This covers situations where the defendant kills someone as a result of...

punching or hitting them

threatening them and causing their death as they escape (eg. running in front of a car)

R. v. Mitchell 1983

In an argument in a post office queue, a fight began...

Don't push !

The defendant punched the old man, who fell against an 89 year old lady, killing her as a result.

Was the defendant guilty of manslaughter, if he hadn't intended to kill anyone? The test was as follows...

1) Was the act unlawful ? (punching someone)

2) Would a reasonable person have realised it carried a risk of some physical harm ?

3) Was the act a substantial cause of death ?

4) Was the act done intentionally ?

If the answer to all four questions was yes, the defendant was guilty of manslaughter

Manslaughter based on Recklessness

This occurs when the defendant was reckless ...

or so negligent, that he did an otherwise lawful act in a way which an ordinary reasonable man would not do ...

The test for manslaughter based on recklessness:

Did your conduct create an obvious and serious risk of causing injury to someone?

Yes

Did you give no thought to that risk, or go on and take it anyway?

Yes

Then you are guilty of manslaughter

Kong Chuek Kwan 1985

Can I ever be guilty of manslaughter for failing to act, or help someone?

Yes, for example in <u>R.v. Instan 1893</u>...

Can I have some food?

No! and I'm not giving you any medicine, either.

The invalid died, while in her niece's care, and the niece was charged with manslaughter

Once you'd assumed care of her, you were under a duty to look after her properly.

Can I be guilty of manslaughter if I don't even touch the victim?

Yes, for example if you threaten them, and they die while escaping from you...

BOO!

...or if they die as a result of shock, from an unlawful act (e.g. burglary)

QUIZ - MANSLAUGHTER

1. Any unlawful act which causes the victim's death, will result in a conviction for unlawful act manslaughter.

   True / False ?

2. A man set fire to his house to his own house, and unintentionally killed his wife, son and girlfriend in the blaze. He wasn't guilty of involuntary manslaughter, however, since he didn't foresee any injury to them.

   True / False ?

3. The defendants picked up a hitchhiker and threatened him while the car was travelling at a speed of 30 mph. The hitchhiker jumped from the car and died as a result of his injuries. What the hitchhiker did was unreasonable and unexpected, but the defendants would still be guilty of manslaughter.

   True / False ?

4. A man points a gun at his friend as a joke. Both treat it as a joke, believing there is no bullet in the gun barrel. Unfortunately, when he pulls the trigger, the barrel rotates round, and he shoots his friend dead. If it was a reasonable mistake to make, will he be guilty of manslaughter?

   Yes / No ?

CHAPTER EIGHT - OFFENCES AGAINST THE PERSON

Assault and Battery are both common law and statutory offences

At common law, to assault someone means to cause them to fear unlawful violence

... even if you didn't intend to carry out the assault

There is no assault, however, if it's impossible to carry out your threat ...

Battery consists of the least touching of another without their consent:

It may even be an offence to strike at someone's clothing

R v. Day 1845

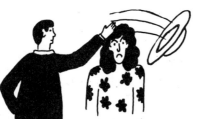

Common assault and battery may only be tried in the magistrates' court

The maximum penalty I can get is six months' imprisonment

Offences Against the Person Act 1861

Section 47

An offence under this section includes any assault occasioning actual bodily harm

"Harm" includes —————— injuries such as bruises or soreness

——— any mental condition induced by the assault

"occasioning" harm can mean harming the victim directly . . .

or threatening the victim which causes them to suffer harm while escaping from the threats . . .

I didn't mean them to take my threats seriously!

It doesn't matter, you can be guilty of assault under s.47 without having foreseen the consequences.

This type of crime is called one of basic intent.

Section 20

This is a more serious offence of maliciously wounding or inflicting grievous bodily harm upon someone.

To "wound" someone under this section, the skin must be broken...

He hit me, and broke my collar bone.

Yes, but he didn't wound you, since there was no break in the skin.

R. v. Wood 1830

To inflict grievous bodily harm, means to cause really serious injury, either yourself, or indirectly,

eg. by frightening someone who's injured while escaping from you
(R. v. Halliday 1889)

or by setting a fierce dog on the victim
(R. v. Dume 1986)

Section 18

This offence is the most serious, and carries a maximum sentence of life imprisonment

J will have committed this offence if J maliciously wound or cause grievous bodily harm to someone.

And unlike section 20, J must show that the defendant _intended_ to cause such harm.

Are there any defences to a charge of assault and battery?

① Consent

He jumped on me, and cut my lip.

Yes, but we were playing rugby at the time.

② Reasonable Mistake

While J was arguing with my mother, he ran and threw me to the floor.

Sorry, J thought you were a mugger.

③ Self Defence

He punched me!

But you were trying to rob me!

QUIZ - OFFENCES AGAINST THE PERSON

① If X points an unloaded gun at the victim, X will have committed common law assault, even if the victim knows the gun to be unloaded.

True / False ?

② A grazed knee can constitute 'wounding' under section 20.

True / False ?

③ The defendant injures a person. If a reasonable person would have foreseen some harm resulting from their actions, but the defendant didn't, an offence will have been committed under section 20 nonetheless.

True / False ?

④ A person can recklessly commit an offence under section 18.

True / False ?

⑤ A threat of future violence can also constitute assault.

True / False ?

⑥ The defendant barred a crowded cinema door, then shouted "Fire!". Everyone stampeded to the exit, and several people were injured. Is the defendant guilty of inflicting grievous bodily harm under section 20, if he didn't touch anyone.

Yes / No ?

A person commits theft if he dishonestly appropriates property belonging to another with the intention of permanently depriving them of it.

Theft Act 1968, s. 1

Actus Reus of theft : Appropriating property, which belongs to someone else.

Mens Rea of theft : Being dishonest, and intending to keep it.

Do I appropriate something if I take it?

To appropriate, means to do anything which interferes with any of the owner's rights over the item.

eg. Borrowing something, and giving it back when it's lost its value . . .

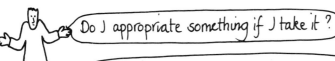

. . . Switching over price labels
R. v. Morris 1983

Here's £10

Being given too much money by mistake, and not telling anyone . . .

Can you steal from someone who agrees to pay you?

Let's see, ½ mile... that's £7 please

Mamma mia!

← overseas student

The correct fare was about 53 pence

The taxi driver committed theft, since he was dishonest, even though the victim allowed him to take the money

Lawrence v. Metropolitan Police Commissioner 1971

Can you steal your own property?

GARAGE

It's my car. I'm just taking it back without paying for the repairs.

The garage owner had a legal right over the car, because of the repairs he'd carried out - by taking it, the defendant acted dishonestly.

The defendant was convicted of theft - of his own car!

R. v. Turner 1971

Are there any defences to theft?

If the person believed he had a right to take the property

But I thought it was mine!

If he reasonably believed the owner would allow him to take it

If there was no way of finding the owner

And some invalid defences...

OK, so I took his umbrella, but I left £5 for it on the table

Appropriation of property will still be dishonest, even if you're willing to pay for it

I didn't steal your lawnmower, I asked if I could borrow it.

Yes, but that was two years ago!

Borrowing something indefinitely can also amount to stealing the property.

Robbery

A person is guilty of robbery if he uses force on the victim, when stealing something...

... or if he puts the victim in fear of force being used

Theft Act 1968, s. 8(1)

Burglary

Burglary is committed when you enter a building as a trespasser, intending to steal, inflict grievous bodily harm on someone, rape, or commit criminal damage.

It also includes someone who enters a place as a trespasser, and then decides to commit a crime once inside.

R. v. Brown 1985

..."entering" a building can include reaching in through a window.

Theft Act 1968, ss. 9 and 10.

QUIZ - THEFT AND RELATED OFFENCES

①   X is owed £10 by his friend. Instead of waiting for his friend to pay him back, X takes his friend's book of an equivalent value. Will X have any defence to theft?

Yes / No?

②   A man picks up and walks off with a £10 note, which he believes he is stealing, but which in fact belongs to him. Has he committed an offence?

Yes / No?

③   X buys a computer from a shop, which he later discovers is stolen property. If he keeps it, will he be guilty of theft?

Yes / No?

④   X picks Y's pocket, then pushes him to the ground as he runs away. Is X guilty of robbery?

Yes / No?

⑤   A woman was given £20 by her lover, to use to buy food. Instead, she spent the money on something else. Had she committed a crime?

Yes / No?

Deception offences involve deceiving someone by words or actions:

such as, selling them a glass ring, and telling them it's diamond

or ordering a meal, knowing you can't pay for it

Obtaining a Pecuniary Advantage by Deception

It's an offence to obtain a pecuniary advantage for oneself or another, dishonestly or by deception.
Section 16(1), Theft Act 1968

What's a pecuniary advantage?

- being allowed to borrow money by way of overdraft

- being allowed to take out an insurance policy

- being able to get money from employment

Obtaining Property by Deception

This is when...

> A person who by any deception dishonestly obtains property belonging to another with the intention of permanently depriving the other of it
>
> (Theft Act 1968, s.15)

A young man needed some money, to go on holiday...

You see, if I don't pay this fine, I'll be sent to prison.

You poor boy, I'll give you the money.

He took the money, bought a car, and went to Spain.
(He was later convicted of obtaining property by deception)

R. v. McCall 1971

This section covers situations such as —— taking money in advance, intending to use it for a different purpose

writing a cheque for goods, when you know you don't have the money in the bank.

The deception can also be by conduct

← imposter

He must belong to the university.

R v. Barnard 1837

53

Other deception offences include ...

Evading Liability by Deception

for example, lying to extinguish a debt   (Theft Act 1978, s. 2)

Making Off Without Payment

But no offence is committed if the person merely forgot to pay.
(Theft Act 1978, s. 3)

Obtaining Services by Deception

for example, having your hair cut, without intending to pay for the service.
(Theft Act 1978, s. 1)

QUIZ - CRIMINAL DECEPTION AND NON-PAYMENT

①   If X leaves a restaurant, intending to pay the next day, X will still be guilty of making off without payment.

                                                   True / False ?

②   A restaurant owner can arrest anyone leaving the restaurant without paying for their meal.

                                                   True / False ?

③   The offence of obtaining property by deception includes someone who attempts to deceive the victim into giving them money, even if the person gives them the money without believing their story.

                                                   True / False ?

④   Obtaining services by deception includes obtaining a free service done out of friendship.

                                                   True / False ?

⑤   The defendant went into a restaurant and ordered a meal which did not arrive. He tried a little of another dish on the table, but left without paying, because he did not like it. Was he guilty of evading liability by deception.

                                                   Yes / No ?

QUIZ ANSWERS

Chapter One - The Nature of a Crime

① True

② False   They can, once a warrant has been obtained, or if it appears that service of a summons is impracticable, or to prevent that person causing injury to himself or another.

③ True

④ False   He may be guilty of attempt, under the Attempts Act 1981.

⑤ False   Not necessarily, they may have a defence which exempts them from liability (eg. self-defence, duress,)

Chapter Two - Actus Reus

① False   Since the wound was almost healed when X was given the wrong treatment, the wound was not an operating and substantial cause of death. (R.v. Smith 1959)

② False   X tried to argue this, and failed - they coincided since it was part of one continuous act. (Fagan v. M.P.C. 1969)

③ False   The shooting was a foreseeable consequence of his act, and did not break the chain of causation (R.v. Pagett 1983)

④ False   They were, since they had voluntarily assumed responsibility to look after her, and should have sent for medical attention.

QUIZ ANSWERS

Chapter Three - Mens Rea.

1. Yes — It was held that ignorance of the law was no defence (R.v.Bailey 1800)

2. False — The mens rea for murder is the intention to kill someone. Murder can still be committed with a good motive.

3. False — When you book an appointment at the dentist, you intend to go, although you may not want to go.

4. False — 'Reckless' can have two meanings : Caldwell recklessness, and Cunningham (objective) recklessness.

5. False — In Thabo Meli v. R. 1954, it was held that the sequence of events could not be separated, but were part of one continuing act.

Chapter Four - The Defences

1. No — X voluntarily joined the gang. (R. v. Sharp 1987)

2. No — His culpability lies in the fact that he continued to drive while feeling sleepy.

3. Yes — As long as X can show he only acted that way because of the alcohol he had involuntarily taken.

4. No — He had voluntarily consumed the drink, knowing it had some alcohol in it. (the decision may be ifferent if the defendant believes the wine to be non-alcoholic)

5. No — The threat must be one of immediate violence.

QUIZ ANSWERS

Chapter Five - The Inchoate Offences.

① True   Incitement is a triable-either-way offence, and may be heard in the Crown Court, resulting in a more severe punishment

② True   Although a person cannot be guilty of conspiring with only his/her spouse.

③ False   You may be guilty of attempting to incite (R.v. Bankes 1873)

④ Yes   Invicta Plastics Ltd v Clare 1976

⑤ No   There is a difference between attempting to do something impossible, and something which is not illegal in the first place (R.v. Taaffe 1984)

Chapter Six - Murder

① False   It can be enough to show an intention to cause really serious harm.

② False   The defences of provocation and diminished responsibility are only available on a charge of murder.

③ False   The defence of provocation includes being provoked by things done, or things said, or both together.

④ False   X would be guilty if the stone hit another person, but the mens rea for one offence (harming a person), cannot be transferred to a completely different offence (criminal damage)

⑤ False   It may be taken into account, if it is a sufficiently permanent characteristic.

QUIZ ANSWERS

Chapter Seven - Manslaughter

① false — The unlawful act must be one which carries the risk of at least some physical harm (albeit slight)

② false — He was guilty of unlawful act manslaughter, since a reasonable person would have foreseen the risk of some physical harm, even if the defendant didn't (*R.v. Goodfellow 1986*)

③ False — If the hitchhiker's actions were very unreasonable, they would constitute a new intervening act, which breaks the chain of causation. (*R.v. Williams 1992*)

④ No — *R.v. Lamb 1967*

Chapter Eight - Offences Against The Person

① false — Fear is the essential element of assault.

② True — 'Wounding' includes breaking the skin, even in a minor way.

③ False — The test is subjective not objective (i.e. if they did it intentionally, or if they were reckless in the Cunningham sense)

④ False — Section 18 is the most serious offence, with a maximum sentence of life imprisonment, and can only be committed intentionally.

⑤ False — The threat must be one of immediate violence.

⑥ Yes — This happened in *R.v. Martin 1881*.

QUIZ ANSWERS

Chapter Nine - Theft and Related Offences

① Yes   X may have a defence under section 2 of the Theft Act 1968

② Yes   Attempted theft (section 1, Criminal Attempts Act 1981)

③ No   Not if he bought it in good faith, without suspecting that it was stolen - (section 3(2), Theft Act 1968)

④ No   The force must be used in order to steal. X uses force on Y after the theft has taken place.

⑤ Yes   She was guilty of misapplying money, given to you to use for a certain purpose, under section 5(3), Theft Act 1968 (R.v. Cullen 1974)

Chapter Ten - Criminal Deception and Non-Payment.

① False   Not necessarily, in R.v. Allen 1984 the court decided that there must be an intention never to pay.

② True   They are making off without payment, under the Theft Act 1978, s.3.

③ False   The deception must be the cause of obtaining the money

④ False   The service must be one which is normally paid for

⑤ No   The court held that he was entitled to see if he liked the dish offered first (Guildford v. Lockyer 1975)

INDEX